A DIFFERENT
LIFE,
PIECE BY PIECE

First published in Great Britain in 2022 by
The Book Guild Ltd
9 Priory Business Park
Wistow Road, Kibworth
Leicestershire, LE8 0RX
Freephone: 0800 999 2982
www.bookguild.co.uk
Email: info@bookguild.co.uk
Twitter: @bookguild

Printed and bound in the UK by Printed and bound by
CPI Group (UK) Ltd, Croydon, CR0 4YY

ISBN 978 1914471 544

British Library Cataloguing in Publication Data.
A catalogue record for this book is available from
the British Library.

A DIFFERENT LIFE,

PIECE BY PIECE

Gentle advice to help
you find greater purpose
and contentment

Prerana Phadnis

INTRODUCTION

CHANGING YOUR THINKING CHANGES EVERYTHING

This book doesn't contain all the answers. What it definitely does offer, however, is advice from someone who passionately believes that starting to think more creatively can set you on the path towards real change. I know from personal experience that consciously shifting your mindset can gradually help you to achieve a more purposeful and more contented life. Some of you may ask, 'What does creative thinking have to do with how I approach life? I'm not a creative person.' But experience tells me that you don't need to be what we conventionally think of as 'a creative person' to harness the power of the mindset I'm talking about, to be able to use it to find your way around a problem or to imagine useful new possibilities. I believe that all of us have an innate ability to think creatively, and that this has huge potential to enable us to bring about positive change in ourselves, our work and in the lives of other people. This mindset is not the privilege of the few – every one of us can benefit from developing it as a practice.

The word 'practice' is important here. Harnessing the power of a new way of thinking isn't easy – changing your habits requires conscious and ongoing effort. So, if you want to move from your existing state to one that feels far more positive, something genuinely has to shift. You will have to make a commitment to work on relearning, reframing and rethinking the facts that have thus far shaped and helped define your life. I hope very much that keeping this book to hand will inspire you to begin and then continue making this effort. My messages of encouragement and the personal examples I use to illustrate the principles they embody have been carefully chosen to help you make the kind of positive changes that should lead towards greater purpose and contentment.

Why do my mosaic artworks (as well as some of my photographs) appear throughout the book? I started making mosaics three and half years ago, after I retired from a 27-year career as a business coach. Since then, mosaic-making has become a bit of a happy obsession, and the thing in my life that allows me to really focus on the 'here and now'. This process of immersing myself in a new-found creative medium has proven to me the importance of many of the things I've advised in this book, including actively trying to create a more interesting life, questioning and pushing traditional boundaries, and allowing myself regular 'me time'. My mosaics are in no way intended to be examples of 'amazing pieces of art' – I am not an experienced artist and I am well aware that I still have a lot to learn. They are included in the book to underline how starting something new can be a really positive force for change in other areas of your life, as well as to help communicate my messages in a fun and playful way, and (hopefully!) to make you smile. (I think we all need to smile more.) The mosaics are also an important part of the journey I've been on in deciding to write a book (something I'd never done before and which I have enjoyed immensely), because making them continues to prove to me that acting on the urge to try something new is always well worth the risk.

1.

BEGIN LIVING A TRULY SUCCESSFUL LIFE

Taking the First Step

This is one of my early attempts at making a mosaic portrait; although I didn't feel I'd captured the likeness of the lady and knew there were lots of other improvements to make, it felt good to have taken the first step.

SUGGESTION

No one is a failure; I absolutely believe that. If you find it hard to agree with me that may be because today's media has had a negative influence – I think that far too much of what we now read, watch and hear is focused on those who have achieved personal wealth and/or fame. If you go around thinking 'I'm not a success and I never will be', then I advise you to reframe what success looks like.

Try defining 'a successful person' as someone who has something to offer other people, who can make a positive difference in the world. I believe that a person's ideas and the service they offer to their family, friends and community are far better ways to weigh their value than the degree of their fame or personal fortune. If you want to make a change in your life, start by asking yourself two questions: 'What is really important to me?' and 'How can I use my core beliefs to make a difference?' Please don't worry about starting with actions that seem small (helping a neighbour or a friend at work with a problem, say) – the most important thing is to take the first step. You don't need to change the world right away!

IN PRACTICE

Through my work with mosaics, I recently met a former solicitor who has a passion for recycling, in particular for finding new uses for plastics and other materials that cause significant damage to the environment. This woman helps spread the importance of the recycling message through making art from entirely recycled materials – transforming what people throw away into something of real value. Her new work moves her away from conventional measures of value and status, but has allowed her to realise very personal goals. But she didn't achieve her artistic potential overnight. This woman had to learn about process, prepare a portfolio of her work, and research ways to present her work to the right audience. All this effort and determination definitely paid off: she is now a full-time Eco-Artivist or 'Rubbish Artist', and her work recently won a competition run by London's Saatchi Gallery.

Making a Living from Trash

When I was in India I saw a young man at the seaside collecting discarded objects to sell for recycling, and wondered at how different his humble use of rubbish was from the way in which some artists in London use it to make artworks.

2.

BELIEVE IN YOUR ABILITY TO BE CREATIVE

It's fascinating, and inspiring, to see how this tree has, over hundreds of years, managed to find a way to live in the harshest seaside conditions, and in such an unusual relationship with a building – this image reminds me that anything is possible.

SUGGESTION

Creative thinking is a powerful tool because the solutions generated by looking at a problem in a different way can lead to real change. But do you have to be a Creative Type to make use of creative thinking? Absolutely not; anyone can come up with ideas. Give yourself permission and you can 'be creative' as a care worker, a project manager or someone who works in a factory or a supermarket – this sort of thinking is not just for the likes of artists, writers or musicians.

What often gets in the way of coming up with ideas are the boundaries that are placed on us as children, and which continue to limit our sense of our own potential. You could, for example, be an accountant who grew up thinking you had no creative ability because an art teacher once told you that you were 'no good' at drawing. But as a financial advisor your work constantly demands the ability to see new patterns and possibilities in a client's earnings, assets and liabilities, and then to effectively communicate your ideas about how best to move forwards. So it's not only in the arts that creative thinking happens – creativity can drive change in more practical spheres, too. Whatever you do for a living, try using the affirmation 'I am creative, and I can bring about change' and see the difference it makes.

IN PRACTICE

In India the colloquial Hindi-Urdu word *Jugaad* is often used to describe the kind of innovative 'work around' thinking that enables people to develop clever on-a-shoe-string solutions to common problems. An example of this approach that I really love is the story of Pandit Ram Chandra Sharma. He was a craftsman who in the late 1960s ran art therapy sessions with patients at a hospital in Jaipur in India who were suffering from polio. Sharma had a restless interest in finding solutions to practical problems; while he was at the hospital he became aware of the plight of the lower-leg amputees who were struggling to afford prosthetic limbs imported from Germany and the United States. The design of these devices also didn't adapt well to use in life in India, making walking barefoot and sitting cross-legged quite difficult.

The far cheaper and more culturally appropriate prosthesis Sharma came up with was inspired by seeing new potential in the rubber of a flat tyre he noticed while waiting for his bicycle to be fixed. Seeing beyond something's current application he imagined how rubber could be used to make a 'foot' that attached to a hinged prosthetic leg made from wood. Working with an orthopaedic surgeon, Sharma developed the 'Jaipur foot', a device that is still the lowest-cost prosthetic limb on the market, and which due to its price (around $40) is a life-saver for a vast number of amputees around world — to date, at least 1.5 million people in 27 countries have been fitted with one.

Kites over Jaipur

As well as being the birthplace of the 'Jaipur foot', the city of Jaipur in India is also known for its kite festival, kites (birds) and the production of vibrant textiles — this mosaic plays on all of these elements to create a 'Jaipur vibe'.

3.

DRAW ENERGY FROM TIME TAKEN FOR YOURSELF

I always enjoy observing people when I'm out and about, and couldn't resist capturing this 'Sleeping Beauty' in the midst of all the hustle bustle in one of central London's garden squares.

SUGGESTION

When you look back over the story of your life, does it mostly make you frown? Without conscious effort it can be easier for us to remember the things that have gone badly for us. But dwelling on negative events makes it more difficult to move forward – you need to look again, dig deeper and realise that lots of things that have happened *are* worth celebrating. Things such as learning to ride a bike aged 40, having the courage to leave a job in which you weren't valued, successfully growing plants from seed when you used to just buy mature plants from a garden centre, making 90 home-cooked meals in a month during lockdown, or finally doing a full headstand in yoga after years of practice.

I find that it's easier to reflect more positively on life in general if you draw on the energy offered by regular 'me time'. At least once a week, actively take time for yourself; do something you really enjoy, preferably alone. It doesn't have to be an organised activity or cost money – simply sitting on a park bench people-watching can be quietly restorative.

IN PRACTICE

Like most people, my journey through life has been characterised by plenty of downs as well as ups: rejection letters, bad job interviews, the guilt of not spending enough time with my family, painful illnesses, numerous surgeries, loneliness. I've learned that although it's important to acknowledge and learn from each of these things, it's more productive to focus on what *has* been good: things such as my getting into Central Saint Martins in London to do a Masters in Industrial Design aged 32 when my children were just 7 and 2 – the course was two years of hard slog but I made it to the end!

I find it's easier to look backwards with a smile when I've topped up my store of personal energy with some 'me time'. My particular form of this is walking around bits of London beyond my own neighbourhood, looking for things that stimulate ideas for new artworks. I deliberately take it all in: the bustle of people on the pavements, the noise of the road works, the contrasting colours and graphics of shop signage, the movement of scraps of rubbish on the road – I make a conscious effort to really *look*. It works for me every time; I return home feeling energised, and more ready to think positively about what I need to do next.

Out of the Blue

When I was on holiday in Nice a few years
ago, I enjoyed some 'me time' on the pebbled
beach below the city's busy main promenade,
selecting stones that I liked; I brought my
collection back from France with me, and they
later inspired the creation of a seaside mosaic.

4.

BREAK OUT OF THE EVERYDAY

Transitions

This mosaic – which depicts a family tree that
includes myself and my husband, and my two
sons and their partners – illustrates the many
benefits of engaging with a rich mix of
ethnicities, identities, cultures and ideas.

SUGGESTION

Even before Covid arrived, we were all living in bubbles defined by our social and work lives. Whether we are conscious of them or not, these bubbles keep us doing familiar things, talking to the same kind of people, having the same kind of thoughts, making decisions in the same kind of way, eating the same kind of meals. Breaking out of an ingrained habit can be a powerful driver for change in other areas, and one of the best ways to start that process is to make the effort to engage with someone who is not at all like you. That person might be from a different cultural background, much younger or older than you, have opposing political views, or work in a job that seems almost the complete opposite of your own. Talking to someone outside of your everyday life will encourage a positive cross-fertilisation of ideas that should enable you to look at your problems differently, as well as to see new possibilities in work, and in life in general.

IN PRACTICE

Back in the 2000s when I was a business advisor working in London, the local chambers of commerce ran what they called 'Sector Clubs'. These networking groups offered small businesses in the same sector (food, creative, logistics, manufacturing, etc.) the opportunity to get together to share ideas, discuss current issues and find solutions to common problems. Although this service certainly had its place, when I attended meetings, I saw that people who found themselves in a room full of their competitors were often reluctant to openly share their ideas. Being surrounded by individuals in the same sector as their own also made it difficult for attendees to see things with 'fresh eyes'.

I proposed that the members of each sector club mixed with those from another, encouraging them to choose one that represented a sector they were not familiar with. This initiative was a real success: business owners gained insights into how things were done outside of a familiar sphere and took positive approaches back to their own everyday work practice. People – particularly men – often found it difficult to work outside their comfort zone, but once persuaded they really enjoyed exchanging ideas with new contacts.

Out of the Mould

This mosaic was produced by using a method
a bit like the one involved in baking an
'upside down' cake; I used mosaic pieces to
decorate forms made by filling discarded
cupcake moulds with watered-down tile
adhesive – bringing new elements into my
normal practice was a useful experiment.

5.

BELIEVE IN YOUR ABILITY TO FIND SOLUTIONS

Fingerprint

The design of this mosaic was based on one of
my fingerprints. I made this piece when I needed
a physical reminder that I have something
unique to offer, and that although it's necessary
to learn from others, it is the expression of my
own ideas that will make my work meaningful
and special.

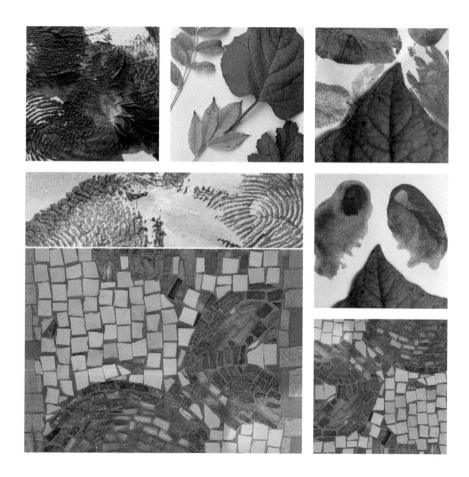

SUGGESTION

If you're feeling negative about where you are in your life, try to stop blaming external influences: your upbringing, your education, the limitations gender may have placed on what you've been able to achieve, etc. And please also let go of thoughts that begin with 'If only...'. You know the ones: 'If only I was taller...', 'If only I had more money...', 'If only I was funny...'. Blame and 'If only's both sap your emotional energy. They also help obscure the fact that, like everyone, you have a unique blend of attributes and skills that can be harnessed to help make positive changes. Shift yourself out of a negative mindset by more generously assessing what it is that you might have to offer, and looking more carefully at where opportunities lie.

Focus on what it is that you want to change (e.g. a job you feel over-qualified for, being creatively stuck, feeling lonely), and see whether you can identify the first steps towards creating your own solution. What are the things that can help you move towards your goal? The skills you could capitalise on, the contacts whose advice you could ask, the activity you could start, the training you could sign up for, the groups you could join, the new job area you could research, etc.? It's fine to start small – any form of action creates impetus and will help the overall task seem less daunting.

IN PRACTICE

In spring 1988 I was living in Palmers Green in north London with my family, and was about to graduate with a Masters in Industrial Design from Central Saint Martins. I wanted to get a job in design with a friendly small business, and one near home, so that I wouldn't be too far from my children. The problem was that most jobs for industrial designers were based in central London, which was a long daily commute away. I realised that responding to job adverts wasn't likely to produce a solution, so I decided to try and create my own. In those pre-internet days, the Yellow Pages directory was the place to go to find local information. I used it to thoroughly research my local area, looking for relevant businesses that were no more than 30 minutes away by public transport from my home.

My efforts paid off: I found a very interesting business only a 20-minute bus ride away that made playground equipment. I invited the company's directors to my degree show, where I convinced them that they needed to hire a designer with young children (after all, they were the company's target audience!). So I got my dream job as an in-house designer, having used one of the limitations of being a mum with young children to help create my own opportunity. I had the time of my life working for Interplay;

the directors also had young children, and my boys both road-tested the play equipment and featured in the company's product brochures.

This image of a little girl playing uninhibitedly with beach sand reminds me that I produce my best work when work feels like play.

6.

ENRICH YOUR CONNECTION WITH OTHER PEOPLE

The sight of these matching tour guides – whom I noticed on a trip I made to San Miguel in Mexico – made me smile; they are in the job of creating a meaningful (although temporary) connection with a group of people, but in this moment looked much more connected to their mobile phones!

SUGGESTION

There's an important difference between conversation and dialogue. Most conversations focus on a basic exchange of facts whereas a dialogue enables you to exchange ideas, opinions and experiences. *Really* talking offers people the opportunity to understand each other better, which has the power to fuel positive change. When speaking to others, especially those you don't know well, it's often easier to stick to the likes of where they live, the kind of product their company produces, what their journey into work was like, etc. But to enable a richer and more productive connection between ourselves and our colleagues, neighbours and acquaintances, we need to go further. It can take a bit of practice, though. For example, it will take a conscious effort to answer the standard 'How was your day?' with something more meaningful than 'Fine, thanks'.

It's also important to give people a chance. For example, any time you think 'He/she is too different from me', try to reframe your thinking, challenging yourself to identify possible common ground, not differences. I assure you that if you do this, there will be something you can think to use as a starting point for a friendly conversation. Make that leap of faith and you should be rewarded by a fruitful (or maybe surprising!) outcome, even an enhanced willingness to celebrate your differences. Possibly the best way to foster more meaningful connections is to practise picking up the phone instead of emailing someone – better still, meet for a coffee or a walk.

IN PRACTICE

A large proportion of the clients I worked with as a development consultant were small family-run businesses. I was asked to do some strategic work in one soon after the boss's son had joined the firm. When I asked how this man was getting on, he answered, 'It's just a job.' This diffident kind of answer is typical of situations when two generations don't see eye to eye. Although the father had run the firm for many years, and was proud of having built it up from humble beginnings, he was getting ready to retire. He had assumed his son would just come in and pick up the reins, needing only a straightforward handover to get up to speed with what would be an unchanging vision on how to deal with staff, logistics, customers and suppliers. As the company's business coach, I encouraged the father and son to have a proper dialogue about what they each wanted. This kind of shift is never achieved overnight. A number of small steps were required, which these two men worked through as they collaborated on the development and launch of a new product. We agreed some ground rules:

1. Say 'We can do this' rather than 'But it won't work'
2. Practise a more inclusive mindset: say 'we' instead of 'me'
3. Withhold judgement
4. Celebrate small successes

Eventually the father realised it wasn't helpful to expect his son to be a clone of himself; doing so was actually detrimental to both his son and to the business. The son realised he had to be more open with his father, and to balance honouring what his father had achieved with not being afraid of trying out his own ideas, even if it meant making mistakes. Over the course of the next year, the two men gradually bridged their differences, enabling them to be able to move forward in a positive manner; a more meaningful way of interacting with each other had led to more mutual respect. Eventually, the father felt able to distance himself from the day-to-day running of the business, and his son was able to go on to significantly grow it with new ideas and new ways of working.

Dialogue

I made this mosaic sculpture using three elements: the base is an old brick that was removed as part of renovation work done on our house, and then facing each other above are two of the kind of breeze blocks that were used to build a new structure in the same project; the piece represents a dialogue between old and new.

7.

DON'T LET LABELS DEFINE YOU

Food Diary

In January 2021 I kept the labels and other elements from lots of the different products I had eaten and drunk over the course of the month, and used them to make a piece that took those wrappers, etc. completely out of their normal context. It was fun to make and made me far more mindful about what I was consuming!

SUGGESTION

Labels act as convenient shorthand, helping us to make sense of the world by organising things in particular categories. But when labels are applied to human beings they can become problematic. If someone gets described (by parents, friends, partners, colleagues, etc.) as 'lazy', 'strict', 'tidy', 'creative', 'the clever one', etc., it has an effect on the way other people see and treat that person. Even if it seems a positive one, any label subtly encourages others to focus on a single element of a person's personality or skill set, and limits their sense of what that individual might be capable of. And it's not only others who stick labels on us – it's often ourselves doing it, sometimes unconsciously. Whoever's handing the labels out, though, they will always restrict a person's potential by suggesting that individual can't be many different things, and doesn't have the capacity to change.

If you feel you've been given a label that's boxing you in, change it – write yourself another role in life's story. If, for example, other people (or you yourself) have given you the label 'the quiet, sensible one', try resisting it, choosing instead to try and be 'the bold, confident one'. External prompts can help: you could try small shifts in your style (experiment with dressing in bolder colours?) or make a conscious effort to try and share your opinions more. Doing things in a new way can often trigger surprising changes – it should encourage people to adjust the way they see you, and you might even start enjoying being the 'new' you.

IN PRACTICE

I don't have many happy memories of my early education, which was at a girls' convent day school in Mumbai. I didn't make friends easily nor show much academic promise. I was usually in a world of my own, branded a day dreamer and a bit of a liar; I had a habit of telling silly stories, about things such as drinking ginger ale and eating asparagus soup (exotic things I had in fact only read about, in books by Enid Blyton!). Playtimes were unsupervised so I sometimes went off on my own, out of the school gates (which were opened to allow the children to buy snacks from street hawkers) to the school next door, to watch another group of children play. This other school felt to me like somewhere I might be more popular and not judged. I don't think my parents knew I was unhappy. I had a younger brother and a baby sister, and my family lived in a one-bedroom bungalow, so to give everyone a break I spent most weekends with my mum's parents, who lived nearby, in a big house with plenty of space. I was spoiled and loved unconditionally by my grandparents, as well as by a number of uncles and aunties. After a miserable week at school, the weekend was my solace.

When I was about 12 years old, I finally mustered up the courage to confide in my parents. At the time my dad happened to be changing jobs so it was a good moment for me to ask for my own fresh start – and it was arranged for me to move school. This was my opportunity to wipe the slate clean, to forget the sneering faces and the unhappy memories associated with my previous school, as well as to drop the labels that had been applied to me there. I was more mature now and my personality blossomed. I started to enjoy school. I made friends, my academic work improved considerably, and I started to do things I'd never tried before, including doing drama and reciting poetry. Over time I became a confident student, eventually excelling in my school leaver's exam and making it to university to do a degree in architecture.

Hanging in There

The intention with this mosaic was to try and express something of the vibe of the city where I was brought up: Mumbai, a place where the only way to survive and to thrive is to have plenty of resilience (and which like all cities in India has huge open-air laundries where people send their family's washing).

8.

DON'T FORGET TO ACT AS WELL AS TO ANALYSE

Wedding

I made this piece when I was thinking about the various commitments I had made in my life, including those made as part of getting married. The design attempts to represent some of the metaphors and symbols that are common across different cultures in relation to weddings, such as flowers, rice, walking down a path, taking the rough with the smooth, etc.

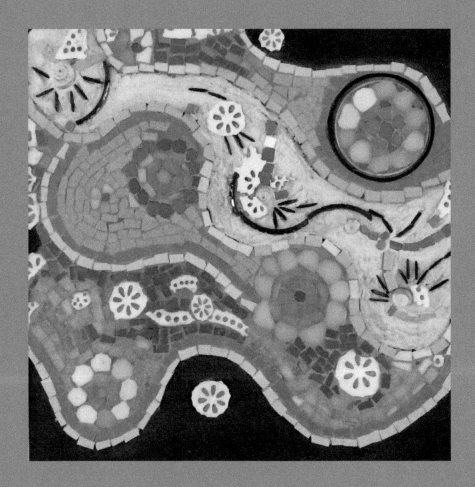

SUGGESTION

There's a well-known saying in business: 'Sales is vanity, profit is sanity and cash is king' that feels worth reframing as advice for when you're trying to make meaningful change. A helpful reworking of this might read 'Analysis is vanity, planning is sanity and action is king.' When you're looking for ways to move on, it's natural to want to spend a lot of time on thinking through what you want. But don't get stuck – once you've come up with some possibilities, pick one or two ideas then focus on ways to realise your goals. The final stage is taking action – the only one in which change can actually happen.

If you've got stuck at either the thinking or planning stage, it's helpful to try to identify what's blocking your ability to take decisive action. It might be a very personal reason, of course, but at least one of the following statements (and their translations!) will probably sound familiar:

- 'Before I start, I need a perfect plan' = fear of failure
- 'I need to get more feedback on that idea first' = fear of taking a risk
- 'I need to finish something else first' = distraction is an easier option
- 'Doing that didn't work so there's no point continuing' = lack of confidence

The resolve to try and overcome the obstacles that hold us back is within every one of us. Remember that *committing* to a certain course of action is always the most important step on the road to achieving your goals.

IN PRACTICE

In terms of my career, launching my own business aged 50 was the best thing I ever did. Up to that point I'd really enjoyed my work as a Design Counsellor and then a Business Advisor's Manager at Business Link for London (Business Link was a now defunct government-funded advice and guidance service for small and medium-sized businesses), but the organisation had begun to change; its services were soon to be offered via an online portal rather than face to face. Staying with them was a cushie option but the part of the job I most enjoyed was meeting business people in person and giving them one-to-one coaching, and the new service was to be both online and far more generic. Acting on my instincts, I decided to take a leap of faith, giving up my 'easy option' job to set up my own consultancy practice (I specialised in helping businesses to think more strategically, and advising them on how to use design and creativity to add value).

Looking back, I'm glad I took this decision, and not

only because Business Link folded a few years later. My business really took off, enabling me to enjoy what proved to be the most fruitful years of my career. Working for myself, I had the freedom to make decisions and take risks that really paid off, with the business moving into delivering contracts on behalf of the London Development Agency and the city's local enterprise agencies.

Optimism

I made this mosaic just before England's second lockdown was lifted. The flower bud surrounded by a rocky landscape symbolises optimism and the promise of good times ahead.

9.

RECOGNISE WHAT YOU HAVE TO OFFER

Discovering

I challenged myself to make a mosaic using only
objects I'd found on the road during one of my
walks, or that had been destined for the bin
– looking differently at what constituted a source
material forced me to come up with new ways
of doing things.

SUGGESTION

When it comes to the way that we think about ourselves, it's easy to get into bad habits. We can get trapped in a negative and limiting mindset, telling ourselves over and over that we have little or nothing to offer. If this sounds familiar, please stop underestimating yourself – doing so is such a waste! I'm convinced that every one of us has *plenty* of useful skills and abilities to draw on, ones we can feed positively into our relationships, work and communities. But before drawing on the potential of these attributes we first need to *recognise* them. This means making a conscious effort to look at past experiences in a new light, and to work out what certain things might indicate about what you are naturally good at.

Try the following exercise: write down everything (big or small) you've done in the last year that's had a positive outcome, and then think hard about what those things might say about you. Make sure your assessment is generous – if you struggle, pretend you're doing it for a friend! For example:

- I planned an adventurous family holiday to a country we had previously never thought we'd go to, and on a tight budget = I'm good at planning, logistics and financial management
- I created a week's worth of healthy and appealing

dinners based mostly on using up everything we had in the store cupboard = I'm a resourceful and creative cook, and know how to save money
- I learned enough French in six weeks to be able to communicate our basics needs when we were on holiday in France = I'm a fast learner, have an ear for languages and can stick at something challenging
- I planned a series of games for my granddaughter's birthday party and everyone had great fun = I understand children, can come up with ideas, and enjoy making people happy.

Turning 'simple' achievements into evidence of your skills and abilities helps force you to reassess what you're capable of. Once you've written a list, try to think about how you can use each of the things these examples illustrate in a different context. Giving yourself more chances to harness what you in particular have to offer will give you more confidence – something that will always leads you out into the world and towards greater opportunity.

IN PRACTICE

During my career as a business consultant I was always keen to find opportunities to help women build the confidence they needed to get a job at management level. In 1994 I was given the opportunity to teach on a 'Women in Management' course, which was aimed at people returning to work after a career break. Each time we ran the course many of the women described themselves in the introductory session as 'just a housewife' – a label I could see was damaging their sense of their own potential. Observing this meant that I began to ask participants on the course a series of questions in our first formal session together:

- Do you manage your family's finances?
- Do you manage squabbles between your children?
- Do you organise family holidays?
- Do you cook meals for others?
- Do you find ways to only spend a certain amount of money each month?
- Do you make important decisions about the children's schooling, health, etc.?
- Do you teach your children to play together and share?

The women almost always answered 'Yes' to all of these questions. My suggestion to them was that all these 'Yes' answers meant that they had very real, valuable and *transferable* skills: they could manage finance, conflict and teams, as well as showing leadership and the ability to make decisions; they were both creative and organised, could plan well and manage budgets. They should think of themselves as not 'just a housewife' but more as a successful 'family unit manager'. I advised the women to remember this way of reframing their experience at their next job interview, and to use it as a foundation for being more confident – they should go in there and smash it! Many of the participants did, getting jobs that put their skills to good use.

I love how in this shot you can see the
sky through the curved architectural shapes;
there's a sense of liberation – a gentle reminder,
maybe, that there is always a way
through things.

10.

BRING MORE MEANING INTO WHAT YOU DO

Fragments of Leaves

This piece honours the humble banana leaf, which is used in southern India for day-to-day meals in place of a plate; available in abundance, biodegradable and offering the opportunity to save significant resources in terms of water, washing-up soap and the production of crockery, it is a simple and yet powerful means of supporting sustainable living.

SUGGESTION

Our lives will always be happier if we can find ways
to bring what we spend our time doing into greater
alignment with what we find meaningful. What aspects
of your work, your family life and your hobbies can you
change to help achieve this? A good way to start is by
writing down and reflecting on the following questions
(I find it always really helps to put something on paper):

- What aspects of my work do I enjoy?
- What skills can I currently offer?
- Can I use these skills to make a difference in
  some way?
- Can I make more of my hobbies, or should I try
  something new?

Use your answers to visualise a more meaningful life,
making yourself its active centre. Then try to draw it, to
capture a concrete sense of what it might look like. It
doesn't matter if you think you can't draw well – this
picture can just be made up of diagrams, stick people,
marks with coloured pencils, things cut out of magazines,
etc. The point is to make your vision of personal change
more real.

Next, write down three areas in which you should be
able to make productive changes. These will of course

depend on what's written on your personal list of skills and things you enjoy, but examples could be:

If you enjoy both writing and travel, consider writing a travel blog as a hobby, and/or offer to write a travel-focused column for the newsletter at your work, or for a charity.

If you enjoy interacting with other people but are stuck in an administrative job, ask for a try out in one that puts you in front of members of the public, or one that relies more on collaboration with others.

If you enjoy cooking and entertaining, think of joining a dining club, or set up your own online.

These notes and the drawing/collage you created should help you articulate your thoughts and lead towards ideas for practical ways to inject more meaning into the way you spend your time. Remember: small changes can cumulatively create a big difference, so don't worry about starting with simple steps – your first change could be as simple as (if you are someone who really values friendship) deciding to make a conscious effort to phone the people you care about more often, or (if you enjoy nature) to start a wildflower area in your garden or on your balcony.

IN PRACTICE

After a number of years of my working at Interplay, a company that designed playground equipment, the directors began to refocus the business, setting up childcare centres for working mothers, mainly for corporate clients. This new direction didn't appeal to me. I needed to find an alternative role that would build more productively on what I'd learned as a designer, as well as fit in with the pattern of my children's school terms. I reflected on my skills and experience: I knew a lot about playground design and equipment, and I also understood interior design and spatial planning. This thinking process produced ideas for two services I could provide on a freelance basis (self-employment offered me the flexibility to work less in the school holidays):

- Designing playgrounds and specifying suitable play equipment for London primary schools, making a point of involving both the children and teachers in helping improve their outdoor spaces
- Developing and teaching my own design module to deliver at local further education colleges as part of their vocational Care Management course

I managed to turn both these ideas into reality. My design service started being taken up by local schools, and having presented my design module to a number of colleges of further education in north London, three agreed to take me on as a visiting lecturer. When I began teaching my design module, the care workers at one of the colleges told me about a particular pitfall in the design of the corridors and reception areas in care homes. They described how although the patterns of squares and circles in contrasting colours used on the floors did help break up the space, they also presented some risks to residents. People with visual impairment often read these patterns as obstructions, even imagining them to be dark holes they might fall into. My design module introduced the students to architectural drawings, enabling them to be more confident in feeding into conversations with architects and designers, and to improve the environment for the residents they looked after. The participants really enjoyed my module because it was very different to the rest of their course and allowed them to bring their creative skills to the forefront.

Bridging the Gap

I am always drawn to images of bridges; as
objects they help me visualise crossing over from
where I am to where I want to be, acting as
a powerful personal metaphor for reaching a
desired destination.

11.

FOCUS ON ACTION NOT ON REWARDS

Frida Kahlo

I made this piece to remind myself of the
importance of focusing on producing work that
allows me to express myself, rather than on
impressing people – Frida Kahlo is always an
inspiration to me as someone who so
energetically expressed things from the heart.

SUGGESTION

Here my advice borrows directly from the *Bhagavad Gita* ('The Song of God'), which is a 700-verse scripture written in the second half of the first millennium BCE, and probably the best known and most famous of all Hindu texts. The *Gita* is framed by a battlefield dialogue between a prince, Arjuna, and his guide and charioteer, Krishna, who is an avatar of Lord Vishnu, one of the three principal gods of Hinduism, and the preserver and protector of the universe. In one part of this conversation Krishna counsels Arjuna on 'righteousness and duty', describing one of the guiding principles Krishna describes we can still apply today: 'Do the very best you can without expectation of the fruit [reward] thereof.' To me this principle feels kind of alien in Western culture, where it seems one is often taught to focus on what you personally want to gain from everything you do.

Many breakthroughs in both the world of art and science have been the result of someone not focusing on 'payback', but purely on *doing* the task in hand in the best way possible. If you absorb yourself in an activity for its own sake, you tend to find more purpose in what you do, as well as more satisfaction. So, adjust your mindset and take action, whether in an existing role or in a new direction. Write, teach, draw, care, listen, organise…

whatever you do, do it with purpose and not for personal reward. There's no substitute for dedication and discipline – the more you work at something, the more confident and competent you will become.

IN PRACTICE

The principle of 'acting without focusing on the potential reward' is one I've applied to time spent on my newfound passion: mosaic making. Over the last few years I've worked very hard to learn the fundamentals of this art form by attending classes led by professional artists. The more I learn, the more I can look back and see I've come a long way – but it's equally clear that I still also have a long way to go. But I don't let this dissuade me; I keep applying my ideas and experiences in the attempt to make satisfying pieces that are meaningful to me (and, hopefully, to other people).

In trying to develop my practice I take part in mosaic-making challenges, without fear of how my work will be judged. I am particularly interested in seeing whether storytelling can work in mosaic form, continually experimenting to see whether the hand-cut pieces of tile and other materials can be combined to express themes, feelings and emotions. I don't know where these efforts will take me, but all my failures teach me something, and I am really enjoying doing something that comes 'from the heart'. I'm not letting the fact that the artwork is imperfect in the eyes of the experts dampen my enthusiasm. Every small piece that I complete is a reason for celebration and provides motivation for my trying to learn more.

Just One Thing
This piece was an experiment on an old tile, using a single colour palette, a snail shell, discarded tile spacers and stone chippings – although I know it's not perfect, I liked how it turned out!

12.

TELL IT YOUR OWN WAY

Walking in the Slow Lane

I made this piece as part of a fundraising effort for a charity called The National Brain Appeal. The story of these three little 'snails' (all made in discarded bottle caps during the first Covid lockdown) is about how slowing down can help accelerate you in other ways, and how in certain ways the smallest of creatures can have the biggest impact.

SUGGESTION

I'm a real believer in the power of stories. As human beings we seem to naturally thrive on being 'told a tale', and tend to more easily absorb information and ideas when they're presented to us in this form. Because they can delight, explain and reassure, stories also create bonds of trust between people – they can operate as bridges between different generations, cultures and interest groups. I'm not saying everyone needs to work at becoming a seasoned storyteller – but I do think it's beneficial for you to be aware of what a more creative way of presenting information can help achieve in your interaction with others.

Reading stories can enrich our store of images and references, and help us find more creative ways to explain ourselves and our ideas. Don't restrict yourself – read anything and everything, including stories 'for children'! Even if you're not actually going to Tell A Story to anyone, it's still useful to practise presenting your thoughts or point of view in a more engaging manner. So don't simply stop at relaying basic information, e.g. 'I went to the supermarket' – try to have the confidence to expand your listener's interest in your experience; you could describe what it was in the supermarket that your eye was drawn to, an unusual outfit a fellow shopper was wearing, or your outrage at the fact that half the vegetables on display seemed to have been flown in from the other side of the planet. Taking the risk of sharing details, observations and emotions will let people know you and what's important to you a little better. This can apply to friends and family, too – there is often much we hold back, even with the people we care about. Elements of storytelling are also worth harnessing in contexts beyond your personal life – work relationships are always conducted far more effectively when people feel they understand a little bit about each other.

IN PRACTICE

My paternal grandmother, Kamala, was (to me, anyway) the world's best storyteller. She'd mastered the skill as a result of doing a huge amount of reading, much of it in English. I still remember how interesting she made the story of *The Merchant of Venice* to me as a young child. She also had a treasure trove of many Indian stories from the Konkan area, which I loved listening to over and over again. Sitting listening to her tell stories are experiences that still feel very fresh in my memory.

During the first Lockdown, I made a conscious effort to hone my own storytelling skills in an attempt to better connect better with my grandchildren, whom at the time I could only talk to over Zoom. I bought an illustrated children's book based on the *Ramayana* (one of the most important ancient Hindu epics), and each week read a chapter to Julius (aged 9) and Indi (aged 7), sharing the pictures with them and adding my own observations. At the end of each session we would recap what had happened in the chapter and the two little ones would then go away and draw characters from the book, such as 'Hanuman the monkey god', 'the vulture who saved the day', 'the ten-headed demon', and so on. Julius and Indi's lively and uninhibited pictures offered me an interesting new perspective on the bit of the story I'd told them, and were often delivered along with intriguing and unexpected questions (many of which I didn't have answers for!). The story-reading was a really bonding experience, and allowed us all to get to know each other a little better.

Stamped in Memory

During the Covid lockdowns we weren't allowed to travel abroad, which made me doubly appreciate looking through my old travel photographs. A piece that celebrates everyday people and situations, this mosaic was inspired by a picture I had taken in India of a man who wore a very colourful turban and sported a striking salt-and-pepper moustache.

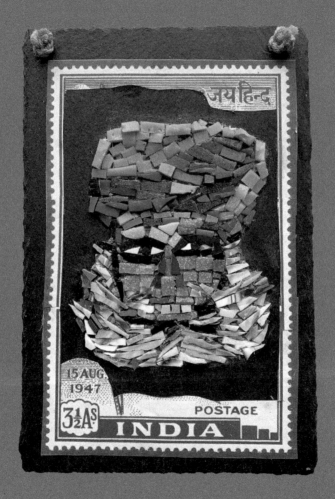

13.

PUT YOUR KINDNESS INTO SERVICE

My Home Today Yours Tomorrow

This mosaic, which I bought from a colleague, is a superb example of campaigning for a cause – against the reduction of orangutans' natural habitat by the planting of trees for the production of palm oil – and thus of sending some kindness into the world (see Orangutan. org for more details).

SUGGESTION

There is a special magic to kindness: it seems that if you put some out into the world, more will soon come back. Regardless of whether or not there's an immediate return, being kind will always make you smile – it's probably the simplest and easiest way to feel good. It's well worth trying, then, to consciously increase the number of small acts of kindness you can introduce into your daily life. Doing so will help you feel more outwardly focused and more connected, and more ready to change as a result. Making an effort to be kind can have a particularly profound effect if your mindset has become rather negative or you're feeling a bit lost – Mahatma Gandhi advised that 'The best way to find yourself is to lose yourself in the service of others'. So although most of us can usually do with being kinder to ourselves, it's important that we also extend some generosity to others. Acts of kindness don't have to be dramatic in scope – it's better to start small because doing so is likely to make your good intentions more achievable.

I suggest that the development of any kindness practice should centre on answers to a very simple question: 'How can I help?' For example, you could help yourself by putting aside some time each week to make a long-delayed start on that online writing course. You could help a friend who over time has developed an unhealthy shopping habit by offering to help declutter their house. You could help the planet by researching how to get the train rather than fly into Europe for your next summer holiday. You could help a stranger either indirectly or directly by, for example, making a donation to a charity or signing up to be an adult literacy coach, or by simply giving the first person you pass in the street the next time you go out a big friendly smile.

IN PRACTICE

A neighbour of mine enjoys sewing. At the beginning of the first Covid Lockdown she was wondering what she could do with this skill (and the little sewing machine that had sat unused in one of her cupboards for so long) to help others. Once it was clear how important face coverings were becoming, she decided to make washable, reusable masks. She gave herself a daily target, and made enough in a month to distribute to around 100 houses in her local area, delivering two through each door. I love the masks she put through my letterbox, especially as their creation was an act of kindness.

This woman went on to make extra supplies of scrubs for staff at the local hospital. As they so often do, her kind gestures had a multiplying effect. Inspired by her actions, I started being kinder to myself and others: simple acts such as making a conscious effort to control my anger, trying to be more understanding, cooking for friends and family, sharing my skills and offering my time to the community through voluntary work. I also started a ritual of phoning an elderly couple whom I knew, and whose son lived on the other side of the world with his family. Each month I rang to ask them how they were getting on in this strange new 'locked down' life we were all enduring. It was a simple, undemanding act but a very rewarding one.

A Kind Gift

Many years ago, I received a silk sari, a kind gift from a friend; over time, the fabric started to look worn, and eventually I couldn't wear it anymore. I loved the sari so much that I decided to make a mosaic based on its pattern, giving my friend's kind gift an extended life!

14.

TRY TO VIEW SETBACKS IN A DIFFERENT WAY

No More Broken

My favourite fruit bowl – a very simple one
made from clear glass – got cracked. Although
my husband had wanted to throw it away, I
resisted the urge to go and buy another bowl,
and used what was left of the old one as the
basis for a mosaic piece made using remnants
of stained glass. Although it's now very different,
it's still my favourite fruit bowl!

SUGGESTION

Whether or not we think of ourselves of 'successful', we have all experienced setbacks – it's not possible to get through life without them. We all react differently when things go wrong, or when we fail. Such events and situations often make people become risk averse, doing anything to avoid future humiliation or disappointment; it feels safer to stop trying. If this sounds like you, I urge you to change your mindset. Given it's certain they will happen, I think that it's sensible to consciously reframe setbacks as an opportunity to learn, as a chance to do things differently.

Begin this change in attitude by reflecting on a recent setback. It might be a rejection letter for a job you really wanted, your child not getting into the school of his or her (or your!) choice, an unfavourable medical diagnosis, a disastrous building renovation job, etc. Take a deep breath and see if you can find a way to take a few positives out of what has happened, or to create an opportunity out of it. With the rejection letter, you could be brave and ask for feedback and suggestions of who else to contact in that particular industry (a direct request for help often wins people's respect). With the worrying medical diagnosis, you could use the opportunity to make some significant positive lifestyle changes, and/or seek support online, maybe making new friends as a result. You cannot change what has happened, but you can try and change the meaning you attach to it.

IN PRACTICE

When I was a postgraduate student at the Indian Institute of Technology in Mumbai, for my dissertation I focused on redesigning the instrument trolleys used in operating theatres. I created a number of prototypes based on detailed research, and when I moved to the UK, contacted several manufacturers of medical furniture and equipment to introduce my ideas. I was delighted when I got a reply from one of the leading companies but was concerned about where to set up a meeting: at the time I didn't have an office, and you couldn't hire spaces by the hour as you can now. In the end, I decided not to worry about appearances and invited two of this company's directors to meet me at home. My very first business meeting in the UK was conducted with my son running around and playing with Lego in the background.

The directors commented on how good my work was, so I was hopeful that the company would agree to the proposal I'd made that I work in partnership with them in order to create an improved trolley design and bring it to market. At the end of the meeting, the men asked me whether they could take away my design documents to share with other directors, to help consider how best to structure our collaboration. In my naivety I agreed. A month later my designs were returned with a note that basically said 'Thanks but no thanks'. Not so long afterwards I saw that slightly tweaked versions elements of my work had made it into this company's product brochure. I felt angry, of course, but I also managed to find a positive in what I'd seen: if a manufacturer of this scale had taken effectively copied my work, my designs must be worth something. Realising this helped me become more confident in my abilities. This encounter also made me realise that I needed to gain some work experience before diving into a business venture, so I went and got a job as an architectural assistant in a multidisciplinary design practice; this new role was a huge help in allowing me to understand how business was conducted in the UK.

Islamic Windows

I bought this group mosaic piece from my colleague Laura Symes. Although its title is *Islamic Windows*, to me it represents 'windows of opportunity' – inspiration for the attempt to learn from my mistakes and move forwards.

15.

ACCEPT THAT LIFE IS NEVER PERFECT

Going for Gold

As a mosaic maker, I'm still learning and often get stuck. In this piece I was unsure how to make the piece look opulent without using expensive gold-leaf tesserae (a glass tile coated with a thin layer of beaten gold), but decided to use gold wrapping paper instead – a happy compromise.

SUGGESTION

From time to time, it's natural for everyone to feel guilt or regret, and the reasons we do range from everyday concerns to the more profound choices that define how we live our lives. People can worry about so many different things: 'not following my diet', 'not spending enough time with the children', 'not giving up smoking', etc. If you're not careful, feeling bad about these things can often lead you to harbour detrimental, generalising thoughts about what these things mean, such as 'I have no self-control' or 'I am selfish'.

If this sounds like you, try to accept that imperfection is part of life, and to stop judging yourself against an impossibly high standard. To overcome negative thoughts about failing to do better, it's important to work hard on finding a happy compromise. It is OK to be 'bad' from time to time – don't punish yourself for missing an exercise goal or for having that chocolate bar because you fancied one. 'All or nothing' thinking can actually stop you making a realistic attempt at achieving your goals – doing so means you're likely to give up because something has gone wrong. Try instead to treat 'lapses' of all kinds as an inevitable part of moving forwards.

IN PRACTICE

It was extremely tough when my mother got diagnosed with cancer. Accepting you can't always physically be there for someone you love is one of the choices you have to make when you emigrate to a different country, but that didn't make the 5,000-mile distance between us (I was in the UK, she was in Mumbai) any less heart-breaking. After we heard the bad news, I felt guilty; I worried that I'd become selfish and worried about not being there for her when she most needed me. I made several trips to India from London during the 18 months my mother was ill. She was always happy during the time we were together, never even hinting that she regretted the fact that both I and my two siblings no longer lived nearby.

Just weeks before my mother passed away, my brother, sister and I were all together with her in the hospital, and she said to us, 'Come on, let's have a photo; I have my three children together. And pass me the mirror, please – I want to look good!' She was all smiles. (I'm so glad we have a record of this very special moment.) My mother's positive and practical attitude helped me accept that the compromise I'd chosen to make between being with her when I could and carrying out my duties to my family and work in the UK was the right one; I hadn't abandoned her, I was simply doing my best to strike a difficult balance.

Kali

To me, Kali, a Hindu goddess, symbolises
female strength – a formidable figure who is not
afraid to destroy negative forces. I made this
mosaic in memory of my mother: although she
was both petite and pretty, she was certainly a
force to be reckoned with.

16.

TAKE A LEAP OF FAITH

Fairy Glens Wedding

I looked in wonderment at this young couple,
braving the cold Scottish weather on top of a hill
in the magical Fairy Glens, Isle of Skye in
Scotland, making that commitment to each other.

SUGGESTION

Thinking creatively about your life and what to do with it always opens up possibilities, but committing to a particular plan can often involve taking a leap of faith. Sometimes you need to make what might feel like a rather risky decision. It may involve veering away from the norm and breaking the rules slightly (or even a lot!), or not being able to base your plan on a proven way of doing things. I think that the most important thing in making any decision is believing in a positive outcome, and to stand by it. Sometimes the best decisions are not ones based on objective evidence but on intuition, or result from a very personal process of weighing up what is best. Although it is always useful to listen to other people's opinions and experiences, ultimately you must learn to listen to your inner voice and decide your own path forwards.

It felt magical: a young couple stood on top of a hill in an area known as the Fairy Glen on the Isle of Skye in Scotland, braving the cold Scottish weather to make a lasting commitment to each other. Always a bit of a leap of faith, marriage, but a wonderful one!

IN PRACTICE

When I was doing my master's degree in London I
needed term-time childcare for the younger of my two
boys, who wasn't yet at school. We had no family in the
UK to call upon. I looked at several options but most of
them required me dropping him off straight after breakfast
to a nursery or childminder, and my son was quite a shy
child, so I wanted a solution where he could remain at
home, in his own environment. We couldn't afford to hire
a nanny, so I reframed my question from 'Where can I
find a babysitter?' to 'Where can I find a mum locally with
a child the same age as my son, and who might need a job?'

I found my answer in the baby clinic where I took my
son for regular check-ups. Over a number of visits I'd
observed another mum called Michelle, who attended the
clinic with her young daughter. I thought she always
seemed to take really good care of her child. Good
nutrition habits are important to me and I noticed that
Michelle never gave her daughter sugary sweets while
they waited, just fruit. One day we got chatting and she
told me she was a single stay-at-home mum; I could see
she might appreciate the offer of a way to make an
income. Going on instinct alone I asked whether she'd be
willing to look after her daughter and my son in our
house. This way each child would have company and

Michelle could take both of them out to the park or the local children's library. My husband also worked only five minutes' walk away, so he could get home quickly if needed. After Michelle's references reassured me she was someone I could trust, we gave her the job. Doing so was a leap of faith but this slightly unusual arrangement worked out brilliantly – it was a win-win for everyone!

Rock Climber

I made this mosaic when I was full of doubt about whether or not to carry on with producing this book. Engaging in artistic activity was really positive and helped bring things back into focus, meaning I was able to visualise the book having been published, which inspired me to renew my efforts to finish it.

ABOUT THE AUTHOR

Prerana Phadnis is a contemporary mosaic artist and retired business development consultant, who spent more than 25 years using creative thinking to help a wide range of companies re-evaluate their growth, innovation, and export strategies.

Prerana moved from Mumbai to London in 1980 and has lived in the UK ever since. Having trained as an architect in India, with post-graduation in industrial design from The Indian Institute of Technology Bombay (IIT Bombay). She gained a Master of Arts in Industrial Design as a mature student at Central Saint Martins (University of the Arts London), juggling her studies with the demands of bringing up two young children. She subsequently obtained a Master of Business Administration (MBA), specialising in innovation creativity and change management while working as a design counsellor at Business Link for London in the early 2000s, which was the largest business advisory service in Europe at the time.

Prerana later set up her own business consultancy, which won several contracts from the London Development Agency. She provided board-level coaching to over 500 small- and medium-sized businesses and she remained a managing partner until her retirement in 2018. Since then, she has dedicated herself to mosaic art. Alongside developing her own practice, Prerana is chair of the board of trustees at the London School of Mosaic, an independent art school that strives to ensure that contemporary mosaic art is accessible to everyone, via public installations and a varied programme of courses.

ACKNOWLEDGEMENTS

Tutors and colleagues at the London School
of Mosaic for allowing me to make mistakes
in mosaic making and learn from them.
www.lsomosaic.com

Family and friends
My husband Sunil for putting up with
shards of glass and an untidy household.
Family, friends, and colleagues for giving
me valuable feedback, and above all
boundless encouragement to carry on.
Special thanks to my brother Raj, my
colleague Lorna, aunt Shaila,nephews
Nimish and Nikhil for their ongoing keen
interest. Thank you, Joy Parker for taking
photos of some of my artwork at the
exhibition in Scotland.

Ally Ireson
For developmental editing.

Jon Allan, TwoSheds
For the design concepts.